D0386107

Welcome . . .

CHARLES MacPHERSON

THE
Pocket Butler

❖❖❖

A Compact Guide to
MODERN MANNERS,
BUSINESS ETIQUETTE *and*
EVERYDAY ENTERTAINING

appetite
by RANDOM HOUSE

Appetite by Random House® is a registered trademark of Random House LLC.

Library and Archives of Canada Cataloguing in Publication is available upon request.

Print ISBN: 978-0-449-01680-0
e-book ISBN: 978-0-449-01681-7

Cover image: © ImageZoo/Corbis
Printed and bound in China

Published in Canada by Appetite by Random House®,
A division of Random House of Canada Limited,
A Penguin Random House Company

www.penguinrandomhouse.ca

10 9 8 7 6 5 4 3 2 1

To my father,
Robert William MacPherson.
Businessman, bon vivant, teacher and raconteur.

CONTENTS

INTRODUCTION

I HAVE SERVED AS MAJOR-DOMO for prominent families around the world, offering household help and staff training services in countless countries. It is my belief that there is no political or business leader, dignitary, king or queen, or movie star who can manage without domestic professionals in the wings. What a really good butler knows are the secrets of the trade that simplify housekeeping and entertaining at home. It's the little luxuries—simple human kindness, decency and attention to detail—that make a dinner memorable or that turn a house into a home.

Following the success of my first book, *The Butler Speaks: A Return to Proper Etiquette, Stylish Entertaining and the Art of Good Housekeeping,* I was consistently surprised by the feedback I received from readers. Although there was great interest in the domestic housekeeping section of the book, the questions I was asked most often related to etiquette and entertaining. I began to see the need for a more compact reference guide that would help readers share in the small pleasures available to all of us. I envisioned a book that would be geared towards young professionals, people who love to entertain and anyone looking to increase their comfort, social skills and knowledge in these areas. And I wanted to write something that would be well-loved and thumbed through time and time again. The renowned cook Julia Child once told me that her favourite part of signing her readers' cookbooks was seeing all the messy, food-splattered pages. She loved knowing that her books were cherished and used often. After a great bottle of wine with my publisher, Robert, we decided to pursue this idea—an easy-to-follow book that would be a definitive and helpful resource that readers could truly make their own. And so, *The Pocket Butler* was born! Because, no matter who you are, you can conduct a more productive social life (and a more productive career, too) with tips and tricks learned from a professional butler.

I consider myself lucky indeed to have worked as a butler for more than twenty-six years. I have had the opportunity to watch the most incredible events unfold within the walls of famous and opulent households around the world. How many people get the chance to witness a dinner in the state dining room of Buckingham Palace? Or stay in the private residence of the renowned Hôtel du Marc, owned by Veuve Clicquot Ponsardin? Or spend hours flying at 35,000 feet in a Gulfstream V with a celebrity? Butlers and household managers work hard, but in return, we are offered rare glimpses of the daily lives of the rich and famous.

But perhaps you're wondering what that has to do with you. As busy working people, you and I have many demands and stresses in our lives that we need to overcome. That's where I come in. Just as you would seek medical or legal help for a problem, I am the professional who has insight into how to make entertaining and manners a natural part of your life. These social skills are the competitive advantages the rich and famous use every day, and you can use them too.

The famous designer Oscar de la Renta (1932–2014) taught me one of the most important lessons of my professional life. When asked, "What is luxury?" his response was this: "Luxury is a feeling." He went on to explain that paying a high price to be served a cup of coffee in a fancy hotel by an employee who pays no attention to you is *not* luxury because it doesn't make you feel special; rather, you leave disappointed. In contrast, buying a cheaper coffee prepared by a vendor who gives you his undivided attention makes you feel appreciated and acknowledged. That is good service. That *is* luxury.

Luxury can be had by anyone at any time, and given to anyone at any time, because it's about making someone feel welcomed, cherished and looked after. And if you can master this concept, success in both your business and personal life is sure to follow.

Charles P. MacPherson

Fewer people seem to realize the true value of proper

ETIQUETTE

and how it can enrich our daily lives and social interactions

W E LIVE IN A TIME when technology is taking over our lives. We used to spend every evening breaking bread with friends and family at the dinner table, but the demands of modern living are such that, for many of us, dinner is picked up from a drive-through window while rushing to a kid's soccer practice. Home entertainment is more about microwaved popcorn and a movie rental, and housekeeping is that Sunday afternoon scramble to do laundry and tidy up before another busy workweek begins. Similarly, rules of social decorum have fallen by the wayside, and fewer people seem to realize the true value of proper etiquette and how it can enrich our daily lives and social interactions. Though we are lucky to have so many amenities at our fingertips, never before has there been a time when we needed professional guidance more—on manners and etiquette, on how to entertain with style and on how to manage our homes in a way that provides a greater quality of life and results in happiness.

Many people feel that having proper manners means being stuffy and pretentious, but I'm here to tell you that nothing could be further from the truth! You can be well-mannered, cultured and a great home entertainer while being yourself—in fact, there's no other way to be. For me, etiquette is not a set of classist rules for rich, famous or snobby people; rather, it's a way of being, based on understanding other people and having consideration for their needs. Letitia Baldrige (1925–2012), the doyenne of American etiquette, once told me her definition of etiquette. She defined it as how we act at the breakfast table when sitting with family; how we speak to the bus driver on our way to work; or how we speak to someone like our mother-in-law when she is driving us a little crazy. What she was suggesting is that etiquette applies to everyone—in any social interaction. Don't worry about memorizing rigid Victorian rules and outdated codes of conduct. Instead, work to adapt these core principles to fit your daily life, whatever that may include.

Modern-day etiquette is about behaving with grace around others, but it serves another function as well: it gives us something to fall back on in new, strange or awkward situations. Good etiquette always takes into account cultural, generational and social differences, and it allows people to handle all situations with civility and dignity. This understanding is paramount for success, because the more you learn about etiquette, and the more you can incorporate these ideas into your daily life, the higher your self-confidence will climb. Now, when I say "self-confidence," I hope no one will confuse that with arrogance (which is, in truth, a *lack* of confidence). Self-confidence that stems from etiquette is ultimately about comfort. It's about putting yourself at ease in any social situation, but more importantly, it's about putting other people at ease. Along with my mother, who taught me how to show respect for strangers, friends, colleagues and family members alike, I had a high school teacher, Mrs. Dorothy Wolfson, who helped teach me how to be comfortable in my own skin. Mrs. Wolfson showed me that my etiquette insecurities made me appear snobbish to others, which was not the impression I wanted to leave at all! By developing my own self-confidence in this field, and learning how to accept myself, I was able to show that generosity towards others, and I am truly a happier person for it. I know that you will be, too.

Etiquette, both social and business, begins with the way in which you present yourself to the world. For that reason, in this section of *The Pocket Butler* we will look at matters of presentation, introduction, entrances and exits, polite acknowledgement, and office comportment, offering tips and suggestions. When you can conduct yourself through these moments with poise, you will accomplish the goal of etiquette: putting others at their ease with respect and thoughtfulness.

THE MODERN GREETING LINE

A few years ago, a client asked me to go to the Middle East to spend some time training his staff. My client's residence has been in the family for several generations and is particularly large, even by my standards—they have several thousand people on staff. In fact, I don't think I have ever worked in a bigger household! While

I was there, I was asked to train the household staff in the tradition of a greeting line. This is a formal reception in which the house staff gathers in an organized manner outside the house to greet guests upon their arrival and to bid them farewell when they are leaving.

Those of you who watch *Downton Abbey* will have seen the staff line up at the main entrance of Highclere Castle whenever a new guest is scheduled to arrive. In contemporary situations, when we think of a greeting line, we likely don't picture anything quite so grand. But, truthfully, a well-composed greeting line could not be more relevant today. You might picture a wedding, with the new couple and their family in a formal receiving line. Now let's think of this in a different way. Imagine your company has invited an important potential new client to your boardroom for a presentation. Making the initial right impression is easy if you have planned in advance how the client will arrive, who will greet your guest at the front door and who will escort him or her to the boardroom. But most importantly, someone needs to think about where all the employees will stand, who on your team will make the introductions and the order in which your team will be presented. These small details are often overlooked, but they make an important impression when done correctly.

ORDER OF PRECEDENCE

There was a time in history when you sat around a dining table in the "order of precedence." Your seat at the table depended on your station or rank in society, and there were well-established rules about who sat where, and why. Today, we may not refer to the order of precedence when preparing for a dinner in our homes, but that doesn't mean we don't apply rules when it comes to seating arrangements.

I think of an order of precedence today as a way of sorting a group of people and finding the most sensible and respectful placement for them around a table. Maybe you're wondering why guests at a table need to be sorted at all? Think about it this way: if you had twelve people to your home for a formal dinner, you'd have to think about who sat where or chaos would ensue. You could end up with a man accidentally seated between his current and former girlfriends. Or you might find a writer seated next to the book critic who just savaged his work in a review! What about a dinner with colleagues at a restaurant? Who sits where, and how is that decision made? And if you have ever organized a wedding banquet, you know all too well how important it is to think about seating, because you want your guests to feel comfortable and at ease with those around them.

For something like a formal international state dinner, rank is still one of the factors that determines seating at the table. Other factors could include the relationship of guests to the hosts and any national or regional customs. North American tables are typically organized so that guests alternate male and female, with the host at one end of the table and the hostess at the other. Ideally, the host will have the highest-ranking female guest on his right and the second-highest-ranking

female to his left. And the hostess will have the highest-ranking male guest to her right and the second-highest-ranking male to her left. The order of precedence will follow in this way down the table. But even if the event you're organizing isn't nearly as formal as a state dinner, putting some effort into a seating plan will ensure that nobody is offended by something as trivial as their place at the table. At a social event, I would recommend seating people so that there is some mingling of generations, but making sure that no one feels stranded without a person of their own age or interest group to talk to. It's also fun to seat people together knowing that they share a common interest. In a business setting, seat people according to company seniority.

RECEPTION PROTOCOL

Not many of us will ever attend an
official state reception, but much
of the etiquette around such events
applies equally to other important
functions. Here are some tips:

- *Be on time:* When it comes to
  important events, there is no
  such thing as "fashionably late."
  Be a few minutes early if you will
  have to check your coat or if you
  don't know exactly where to go.

- *Do not over-work the room:* A formal event is not for
  promoting your new business or rallying support for a
  cause. Use the event as an opportunity to get to know
  people, and contact your new connections to discuss
  specific matters after the event is over.

- *Never ask for more food:* Asking for a second helping of
  something will draw unwanted attention. Large events

are generally planned down to the minute. By asking for more food you may upset the timing of a dinner, and insult your host or hostess.

- *Connect with your host and hostess*: Make an effort to speak with your host and hostess. Remember to take only a few minutes of their time. If you monopolize your host at a state reception, an official may politely invite you to enjoy the rest of your evening and point you to the dance floor. At a less formal function, you might just find the other guests giving you sour looks!

- *Leave gracefully*: If there is a guest of honour, note that his or her exit is your cue to do the same. Finish one last dance, or cocktail at the bar, then say your good nights and head for the door. If there is no guest of honour singled out, be sensitive to the cues that the party is winding down.

A NOTE ON NOTES

There was a time, long before e-mails, when personal, handwritten correspondence was common. Every proper household had official stationery, and butlers and other heads of staff used this to correspond with tradespeople, as well as for thank-you notes and other household-related communications. I love this old-fashioned custom, and I believe that in our fast-paced world, one way of really connecting with someone is to turn back to tradition and offer something personalized—a handwritten thank-you card, a follow-up note or an invitation. Just as handwritten notes are falling out of fashion, so is fine stationery. Still, I advocate a return to this tradition, too. E-mails simply cannot compete with the beauty and elegance of a card or note. A handwritten note is appropriate to thank a host or hostess for their hospitality, to send thanks for a gift or to express condolences or congratulations. Try in each case to add a personal touch.

See some examples on the following pages.

THANK-YOU

You will never go wrong by sending a thank-you note, and you may even be (silently) criticized for not sending one. So do make the effort to show your true appreciation and make the recipient feel valued!

CONDOLENCES

This is one of the most difficult notes to write. People often don't know what to say to help alleviate the pain of mourning a loved one. I completely understand that sentiment, but this is one note you really need to write. I find that the best thing you can do is to write from the heart. Also, sharing a reminiscence about the deceased person can really help with the bereaved person's grief.

CONGRATULATIONS

Who doesn't love a note congratulating you for a milestone you are celebrating or a job well done? Because of the lack of notes today, these make even more of an impression and are that much more important as a tool of communication.

CLARENCE HOUSE

123 Grosvenor Square

London

April 23, 2015

Dear Aunt Marie,

I wanted to send you a quick note to tell you how very thrilled I am with the news that you bought us theatre tickets for my upcoming 18th birthday! As you know, I love the theatre and hope to major in the subject when I go off to university next year. I hope you will let me take you to my favourite coffee shop after the show to express my gratitude and give us an opportunity to catch up more.

I'm so excited and can't wait to be with you on this special day next month! Thank you for this perfect gift.

Love,

Judy

CLARENCE HOUSE

123 Grosvenor Square

London

April 23, 2015

Dear Carole,

I am so sad to hear of the sudden loss of your mother last week. I very much regret that I was out of town on business and missed the funeral. I have the fondest memories of your mother and the jokes she used to tell us at the table when I would join you and your family for dinner in the backyard. In fact, thinking of them now still makes me laugh. Thank you for sharing your mother with me; she has brought many happy tears to my eyes.

I am going to call you in the next week to suggest a visit. However, please know that if you are not ready to see me, I will not be offended and will wait patiently until you feel like having company.

With much love,

Susan

CLARENCE HOUSE

123 Grosvenor Square

London

April 23, 2015

Dear Bill,

Congratulations on your new job! It must be so exciting to have received this promotion and become the manager of the hardware store, after being there for only three years. I know that every time I need something for my house, your store always has it in stock, and that is a much-appreciated time-saver!

I hope that you and Gayle can join me for a glass (or two) of champagne to celebrate your promotion on Friday evening, at 6:30 p.m. at my house.

Look forward to seeing you at the store in your new role.

Best wishes—

Jane

SENDING YOUR NOTES

In addition to fewer written notes, I have noticed many people who do not know why it is important to stuff an envelope in a particular way, or how to do it. The objective with this task is that when the envelope is opened by the receiver, he is able to read the printed material easily, without having to twist and turn the contents.

THE FLAT CARD

This type of card should go into the envelope with the contents of the card facing the back of the envelope.

THE FOLDED CARD

The folded edge should be aligned with the bottom of the envelope, with the front of the card facing the back of the envelope.

THE THREE-FOLD LETTER

A normal business letter is always folded twice, giving you three parts. Start with the letter facing up on the table. The bottom is folded first upwards one-third of the way, and then the top of the letter is brought to face the bottom. Place the letter into the envelope so that the bottom fold goes to the bottom of the envelope, with the face of the letter towards the back of the envelope. When the reader removes the piece of paper, he or she will be able to unfold it and immediately read the text on the page.

STEP 1

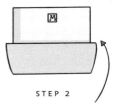

STEP 2

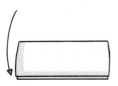

STEP 3

STEP 4

THE LANGUAGE OF THE BUTLER

No matter how many times you may have heard this, I believe it bears repeating: "You have just one chance to make a first impression." When you see someone for the first time—a future employer, a blind date or an anchor presenting the news—you immediately form an impression of that person, be it positive or negative or neutral.

This impression is made within seconds of two individuals meeting and is extremely difficult to change. Fair or not, that first feeling is based on countless tangibles and intangibles, including physical appearance, body language, attitude or even a written communication.

Here are a few pointers that every butler knows to help create a good first impression.

• When meeting someone for the first time, repeat his or her name in your conversation.

- Use the appropriate amount of formality depending on the circumstance—the way in which you are introduced will hopefully provide you with clues—but whenever you're uncertain, err on the side of being more formal, at least at first. Most people will tell you if they'd prefer a less formal style of address, but few will tell you when you've erred and gone too informal.

- Listen carefully when you meet someone, not only to the words a person uses but also to their underlying meaning. Respond when appropriate, and be generous and gracious.

- Always maintain eye contact.

- Be careful of using humour. If you are meeting someone for the first time, you do not want to offend them.

- Check your ego at the door. Wait until you have established credibility before you even consider challenging someone you've just met.

- Choose your words carefully because, rightly or wrongly, what you say will be used to judge your intelligence, education, cultural development and abilities.

BODY LANGUAGE

Imagine you are one of two people applying for a job. As the first candidate interviewed, you stand tall, you offer a firm handshake, you look the interviewer in the eye and you smile confidently. The second candidate, however, has a slumped posture, pulls his hand away too quickly during a handshake and looks at the ground when others speak. Even before either candidate has said a word, an impression has been made. As Candidate 1, you've set the right tone, whereas Candidate 2 is already sending the message that he can't handle the job.

A good butler has much to teach us about how to make a good first impression. He knows that body language is an important, non-verbal part of communication, as are gestures, poses, movements and expressions. As he stands by the door, answers the phone or goes about his daily chores, his voice, posture and manner exemplify calm dignity. Think of this as a recipe for first-impression success, no matter what the circumstance.

WRITTEN LANGUAGE

First impressions are not always made in person. As often as not, you will meet a new colleague or client by e-mail long before you make their acquaintance with a handshake.

E-mail

As wonderful a tool as e-mail is, I find that if not used correctly, it is guaranteed to cause misunderstandings and incorrect interpretations of the original message—and this is never more important than when making a first impression. When communicating via e-mail, keep it brief, on topic and specific. If the issue is particularly complicated or if you are dealing with an emotional situation, then the rule of thumb should be to address it by telephone or in a face-to-face meeting. Tone of voice is tricky to discern when it comes to e-mail, and by allowing someone to hear or see you in the midst of a difficult discussion, you have a far better chance of getting your message across clearly and without incident.

Text Messaging

A text is the perfect tool for quick, short pieces of information, such as "I'm running 10 minutes late" or "Dinner reservation confirmed. Bruno's, 6 p.m." It doesn't work well for long conversations, or with anyone who isn't a close friend. And it never replaces a proper note when one is required. If you need to thank Aunt Anne for the birthday present, it cannot be done via text. Send her an e-mail or handwritten note to express your gratitude, and family gatherings will be far more pleasant!

In the business world, I am not a big believer in texting clients or colleagues. I think it is much nicer and more polite to pick up the phone and call to say you are running late, or to express excitement over a great meeting or project. A text sent in a professional setting runs the risk of looking hasty and unpolished, especially if compared to someone else's well-composed e-mail.

TELEPHONE LANGUAGE

In this day and age, most of us know the basic rules for how to comport ourselves during an important telephone call: speak clearly and audibly, don't chew food or gum, be engaged and listen to the speaker, and so on. But I have found a new challenge  when it comes to telephone etiquette, and that is the conference call.

When you have a medium-sized or large group of people on a conference call, it is important to remember that when you speak, the other participants may not recognize your voice, so it is always appropriate to introduce yourself quickly, with something like, "Charles here. I think the meeting should be held on Tuesday at 2:00 p.m." This correctly identifies you and avoids anyone asking or thinking, "Who is that person?"

A common but major faux pas when it comes to conference calls or long-distance meetings is talking or typing with the phone's microphone turned on. It distracts the other participants on the call and, moreover, can give the impression of rudeness or boredom. If you must type or speak to someone while you are on a conference call, be sure to mute your telephone first.

Video Calling

In addition to an awareness of how you comport yourself on the telephone, you also need to pay particular attention to video calls or conferences. If you are calling a client on Skype or through Google, you absolutely must put some forethought into both your appearance and that of your office. If you work at home and don't generally wear makeup, you might consider a bit of lipstick ahead of time. Think of what you're wearing, as well. Pyjamas are perfectly fine if you don't need to interact with anyone else while working, but make sure to change if a client will see you during the meeting. Lastly, be aware of what is visible in the background. Tidy up the papers you haven't yet filed, or make sure to close your office door if your cat has a tendency to come in and wander over to your keyboard.

POSTURE

A butler's appearance and demeanour is important at all times. His or her conduct, work and stance will be viewed and judged by employers and fellow employees. In fact, posture and stance are important to any professional, and you will always look more polished and poised if you stand up straight. The person who is slumped over is considered sloppy, while the person who stands tall, hands behind back, is considered attentive and professional. There are many business situations in which posture is important, and while the basic rule of standing straight always applies, here are a few tips for specific situations.

AT A CONFERENCE

Something that I learned from my good friend Pamela Eyring, president of the Protocol School of Washington, was where to place your name tag. When attending a conference or large meeting, most of us automatically put our name tag on the left side of our chests, over the heart. But this incorrect! It is highly important that you always wear your name tag on the right side of your body. Why? Because when you shake hands, the right side of your body naturally moves forward. The name tag remains visible to the other person, and helps them see—and, more importantly, remember—your name.

AT A COCKTAIL PARTY

When holding a beverage, try to keep it in your left hand; this keeps your right free for handshakes. Also, remember that it can be awkward to have to shift your drink from one hand to the other while in a crowded room, so it's best to get into this habit early. This trick also works well for purses and handbags. Keep your clutch in your left hand, or under your left arm, and you'll be far less distracted by it over the course of the evening. A great way to see this trick in action is to take note of Her Majesty Queen Elizabeth II, who always keeps her handbag on her left arm so that she can shake hands easily with her right. Trust me, take a look the next time you see her in the media, and you will see how well it works!

GREETING GUESTS

EXPECTED GUESTS

When answering the door, maintain an upright posture, be polite and greet guests with a warm smile. Help them with any coats, winter boots, umbrellas, et cetera, and know what you're going to do with these. There is nothing worse than meeting a guest on a blustery winter day and saying, "Oh dear. I have no idea where to put your coat and boots."

UNEXPECTED GUESTS

When I was a child, sometimes my father would take me to visit friends he hadn't thought to call ahead of time. The two of us just showed up out of nowhere, and I occasionally sensed that we were intruding at the wrong moment. I must admit, it wasn't until I was in my first apartment that I realized how much I dislike unannounced visitors. I found it disruptive and rude to have people drop by out of the blue.

So what do you do when someone arrives unexpectedly? Well, two wrongs don't make a right, so first, be polite, greet the guests and say how happy you are to see them. But remember: it is okay to say politely, "It's so nice to see you, but I'm sorry, this is not a good time." Don't feel obliged to receive guests when it is not convenient. Here are some gracious things you might say to well-meaning but unannounced visitors:

- *"Thank you for stopping by. It means a lot to me, but I'm in the middle of something personal. Can we get together later this week?"*

- *"I'm so glad to see you, but I am just about to go out the door. Let's call each other over the next few days and do that dinner and movie we've been talking about."*

- *"I'm so glad you came by, but to be honest I'm not feeling well today. My plan is to spend the day in bed reading and resting. I hope you don't mind that I call you next week and we can set something up?"*

DOORS AND DOORWAYS

In times gone by, it was customary for men to open doors for women, whether at the front entrance of a private home, at a restaurant or at a shop. This was as true for strangers as it was for family. A husband, for instance, would open the door for his wife if they were both entering the building together; similarly, if a man arrived at a shop at the same time as a woman he didn't know, he would open the door for her to let her pass through first.

Today, in public settings as well as in private ones, you'll see a lot of doors slamming in people's faces—male and female! In my opinion, it is rude for a man or woman to not take a few seconds to hold a door for someone. Chivalry is still alive and appreciated!

HOW TO OPEN A DOOR
FOR A STRANGER

Whether you are male or female, it's polite to open a door for someone if you are both entering an establishment at the same time. So, how do you do this without it being awkward? If you are approaching a door at exactly the same time as someone else, avoid running ahead to get to the door first. Instead, keep your pace even, and when you arrive at the door, simply say, "I've got it," and reach for the door handle. As you open the door, step aside and hold the door wide. This allows the other person to pass through easily. If you don't step aside, the person stepping through has to step around you first, and most doorways are built for one, not two! A polite person will always say "Thank you" to the person who holds the door open, and you may respond with "You're welcome." Once the person has passed the threshold, you may follow.

HOW TO OPEN A DOOR FOR A COMPANION

This happens all the time: you are walking side by side with a business colleague or friend and you arrive at a closed door. Who should open it, and how should this be done without one person crossing awkwardly in front of the other and interrupting the natural flow of conversation? I lean towards the traditional rule where a man and woman are involved, which calls for the man to open the door. But regardless of who opens it, there's a correct way. The person closest to the door who can use his or her right hand to open it should be the one to move forward first. This avoids the "awkward cross." The one exception is if your companion requires assistance (such as an elderly person, or someone with luggage), in which case it is polite to excuse yourself for walking in front of your companion, open the door and allow him or her to pass through.

CARS

As a butler, my interaction with guests began at the moment of arrival and concluded after the guest's departure. If you are a guest at a hotel that has butler service or a car valet, or if you are lucky enough to be invited to a fine home with such service, you should know a few things about how front-door greeting works.

As your car drives up, the butler or car valet will approach the car. He or she may not immediately open the car door. Instead, the good butler or car valet will discreetly look into the car (if the windows aren't tinted) to see if you are ready to get out. For your part, remember that you don't have to rush. If you are on the phone, finish your call before you step out. Take the time to gather your belongings and collect yourself. If the butler or car valet opens the door before you are ready to emerge, simply let him or her know that you need a moment. Your car door will be closed again and opened only when you signal that you wish to step out.

When you are departing a fine house or hotel, the

butler or car valet will try to anticipate your needs by having the car supplied with chilled bottled water, a newspaper and other appropriate amenities. Don't be shy. If there's something you need, ask for it. A good butler will always help you into the car and then, if you are not driving yourself, signal to the driver that you are ready to depart. You can tell the experienced from the inexperienced butler or valet by the way they signal the driver. A knock on the hood of the car rather than a tap on the window is considered unprofessional, because the sound travels inside to the passenger.

In a social situation, it's a nice touch for a man to open the car door for a woman; however, in a business setting, it's best to let a woman open her own door. Either way, if the woman is wearing a dress or skirt, it's a polite gesture for the man to offer to slide into the back seat first. Why? If you don't know, that's because you've never tried to slide across a back seat while wearing a skirt! Any woman will tell you that it's a challenge to do this gracefully, and a gentleman who quietly says, "Perhaps it's easiest if I get in first?" is saving the woman from awkwardness.

PASSENGER ETIQUETTE

If you are a guest in someone's car, be respectful. Don't change the radio station, adjust the heat setting or, heaven forbid, light up a cigarette. If you are uncomfortable with the temperature, politely ask the driver to change it. You can adjust the seat if necessary, though.

Also, if you are driving a guest in your car, remember that there's nothing worse than feeling unsafe in someone else's vehicle. Drive cautiously and alertly. If for any reason you need to slam on the brakes or swerve to avoid a collision, apologize to your passenger. Avoid the temptation to insult, swear or complain about other drivers—unless, that is, you're on a mission to never drive these guests anywhere again!

MAKING INTRODUCTIONS

Making introductions correctly is crucial, and this has nothing to do with old-fashioned manners and everything to do with making potentially uncomfortable situations simple and stress-free. Introductions used to be much more formal than they are now. Over time, the rules have relaxed. Now, most introductions go as follows: "Harry, this is my friend Sally." My belief is that this relaxed way of introducing people has become the norm simply because we don't know what else to do.

There are situations where this kind of informal introduction isn't appropriate, and a few simple guidelines can help everyone involved feel more at ease. Here's how to become the master of the introduction.

1. Introduce the person of lesser status to the person of higher status. Status may be based on rank, order of precedence or age. Here are some examples:

   - In a business setting, the junior employee is introduced to the senior employee, regardless of gender or age.

   - In most circumstances, the younger person is introduced to the older person.

   - In social situations, the man is generally introduced to the woman (regardless of status).

2. For introductions involving multiple people, mention the name of the most important person first.

3. When introducing dignitaries or other distinguished people, use the word "present" instead of the word "introduce," as in, "Your Grace, may I present Mr. MacPherson?"

4. If dignitaries are not present, but you would still like to introduce people formally, you may do so in the following way: "May I introduce to you Mr. MacPherson from Canada?"

5. Dorothea Johnson, founder of the prestigious Protocol School of Washington, advises that when making formal introductions, one should never say, "John, may I present *you to* Carol?" The correct phrasing is, "present *to you*." She offers a clever way for us to remember the difference. Think of the rock band U2. Rock bands aren't known for their etiquette, so this order is incorrect. "To you," unlike the band name, will always be correct!

6. Correctly pronounce names and use correct titles. This might require a bit of research in advance, but it will unquestionably be worth it.

7. Make eye contact.

8. Smile and speak in a warm and friendly tone.

9. Speak clearly.

Making introductions can be intimidating. If you're unsure of etiquette, practise at home, over and over again, until you know the basics. You want the correct words to roll off your tongue. Proper introductions are probably not something you'll ever be complimented for, even if people do admire your grace and style. But if you get an introduction wrong, believe me, people *will* notice . . .

THE DO'S AND DON'TS OF A HANDSHAKE

The handshake is a key point of etiquette because it's an important aspect of making a first impression. A badly executed handshake, poorly timed, will inevitably create a negative impression. You have probably experienced a handshake by a "bone crusher." This happens when a handshake is performed with such force that it actually hurts. This kind of greeting does not show dominance, as some people believe; rather, it makes the person executing the handshake look like a callous idiot. The footballer who is introduced to a ballerina and who uses  a "bone crusher" handshake is not endearing himself to the dancer. Quite the opposite, in fact.

So, what makes a handshake effective? It should be genuine and friendly; it should not be tentative or indifferent. The palm should be warm and dry, not cold and clammy. If you do have clammy hands, keep them out of your pockets so that air circulates, and carry a small handkerchief in your right hand that you can subtly pass to your left hand behind your back before you shake. Remember: your grip should be firm and strong (but not bone-crushing!); it should not be limp and lifeless. Balance is the key to a good handshake.

THINGS TO REMEMBER WHEN SHAKING HANDS

- Maintain eye contact. (This is a Western approach. Remember that in Asia and Africa, eye contact is often considered disrespectful, so don't be offended by this cultural difference, and adapt your approach to the context.)

- Smile warmly.

- Focus your attention on the person to whom you're being introduced or who is being introduced to you.

- Listen to what the person in front of you is saying.

- Keep your hand open and connect "web to web" (palm to palm).

- Gauge the duration of the handshake by paying close attention to the other person. A good rule of thumb is to pump your hand three times or for about three seconds.

WHEN TO SHAKE SOMEONE'S HAND

It's important to know when to shake someone's hand—as well as when not to. A good rule of thumb is to offer a handshake more often than not. In business, this includes the following situations:

- Meeting co-workers for the first time—both upon greeting and saying goodbye.

- Being introduced to new business contacts.

- Congratulating someone.

DO NOT OFFER A HANDSHAKE WHEN:

- The person you wish to greet is of a higher rank or position. Wait for this individual to offer his or her hand first.

- Beginning an interview. Follow the lead of the interviewer.

- The other person has their hands full.

- When travelling internationally, beware of local customs and cross-gender contact. Always take the lead from locals.

Because of fears over the transmission of viruses, there are times, for example during a bad flu season, when people may feel particularly uncomfortable shaking hands. In fact it may have people running for the hand sanitizer. (If you're the one concerned about the spread of germs, remember to run for the hand sanitizer discreetly.)

THE FIST BUMP

Ever since Howie Mandel, a great Canadian and self-proclaimed germaphobe, started offering a fist bump instead of a handshake, this new greeting method took off. In fact, fist bumps are said to reduce the spread of germs by up to 90%, which is welcome news in cold and flu season! When doing the fist bump, simply touch knuckles together with closed fists, with little or no force.

HOW TO OFFER YOUR BUSINESS CARD

The etiquette for handing out a business card is just as important as that for shaking someone's hand. While business card etiquette is much more relaxed in Western cultures, it is still important to be respectful in how you approach this exchange.

The more formal Asian method of offering a business card with two hands is becoming more common around the world. What I find interesting is that when you use this method in the West, people are impressed. It makes you appear both worldly and knowledgeable to use the formal style. Follow the protocol below and you will never go wrong.

In some cultures, the business card is considered a representation of the owner and therefore should be treated with respect. Make a point of reviewing the card and commenting on it before putting it away.

Do not offer your business card using just one hand. This is considered arrogant and suggests that the information on your card is unimportant.

Do not offer your business card holding the bottom of the card. This is awkward for the person who receives it.

CUBICLES

When Robert Propst of the famed Herman Miller office furniture company designed the cubicle workstation, it was meant to offer a productive way to move teams around during project-based assignments. Today, the office cubicle is a staple in most businesses, and never moves. As forward-thinking as Mr. Propst was, I don't think he ever imagined the etiquette issues his office designs would create. Below are my top tips for courteous cubicle behaviour:

- Be aware that others can hear you, and do your best to keep your personal noise to a minimum.

- Never borrow items from a co-worker's cubicle without asking first. Just because the area is open to passers-by doesn't mean that its contents are up for grabs.

- The cubicle isn't a place to paint your nails or walk around in your socks. Don't pass items over a cubicle wall, either. Remember that your privacy is limited, and don't do anything you wouldn't be comfortable with the CEO seeing!

- Many people eat lunch at their desks nowadays, even though this is generally considered a lapse in etiquette. That being said, if you do eat at your desk, be aware of food odours and be considerate of your neighbours who may not appreciate the leftover smell from your lunch. For the same reason, be sure to dispose of your garbage in the common lunchroom rather than in the personal garbage bin by your desk.

- Even though cubicles don't usually have doors, remember that it's someone's personal space. You'll never go wrong by knocking and waiting to be invited in, and always ask before taking a seat in the guest chair.

- We all love a space that reflects our personality, but make sure your personal items, such as photographs and knick-knacks, do not overwhelm your cubicle area. Yes, it's your office, but in a business environment it's better to err on the conservative side.

- Never, ever eavesdrop on others' conversations. It is not only rude, it also makes people feel highly uncomfortable. Regardless of whether the conversation is a business or personal one, do your best to block out the information and respect your colleagues' privacy.

HOW TO CALCULATE A TIP

Tipping is a social custom that varies throughout the world, and I am constantly asked how to determine what the correct gratuity should be in different situations. I've compiled a chart on the next page to help steer you through some of the most common circumstances where a tip would be involved.

BUTLER'S TIP

If a doorperson hails a taxi for you
from a residential building, there is no
need to tip him or her. But do tip if you're
leaving a hotel or restaurant.

TIPS BY COUNTRY

	North America	UK	Europe
Restaurants	15–20%	10–15%*	10–15% *†
Bellman	$1–2/bag	£1–2/bag	€1–2/bag
Housekeeping	$2–5/day‡	£1–2/day‡	€1–2/day‡
Room Service	10–15%*	10%–15%*	10%–15%*
Concierge	$10–20/request *depending on the service provided*	£10–20/request *depending on the service provided*	€10–20/request *depending on the service provided*
Doorman	$1–2 *for hailing a cab*	£1–2 *for hailing a cab*	€1–2 *for hailing a cab*
	$1–2/bag *for carrying luggage*	£1–2/bag *for carrying luggage*	€1–2/bag *for carrying luggage*
Taxis	10–15%	10–15%	10%
Hairdresser	15–20%	10%	10%
Tour Guides/ Drivers	15–20% of excursion	10% of excursion	€2–5/person
Valet Parking	$2–5 *when car is returned*	£1–2 *when car is returned*	€1–2 *when car is returned*

* if no service charge is included

† A 15% servis compris is generally included, though it's okay to leave extra (up to 10% in cash)

‡ with a note written "Housekeeping – thank you" and left in an obvious place

Japan	China	Hong Kong
None	None§	10–15%*
None§	¥5–10/bag	HK$10–20/bag
None	¥10–15/day	HK$10–20/day‡
None	None	10–15%*
None	None	HK$20–50/request *depending on the service provided*
None	None	HK$10–20 *for hailing a cab* HK$10–20/bag *for carrying luggage*
None	None	Not expected; round up
None	None	10%
¥2500–5000 (10%) *for a private tour guide and half that amount for the driver§*	¥80–150 *for a private tour guide and half that amount for the driver§*	HK$100–150 *for a private tour guide and half that amount for the driver*
None	¥5–10	HK$10–20 *when car is returned*

§ Though tipping is not customary there are a couple of occasions where it is accepted i.e. full-service traditional inns and high-end restaurants. Always place the tip in a small envelope and present it discreetly. Handing out money without an envelope is considered impolite. For guides and drivers, tip should be given at the start of the day.

There are two important rules to follow when **ENTERTAINING:** Make sure every-one has a drink in hand and some-one to talk to.

PEOPLE MAY BE UNSURE when it comes to entertaining because they simply don't know what to do or how to conduct themselves. I find it helpful to remember the purpose of etiquette: *to show respect to others.* This is true when you're entertaining and when you're a guest in someone's home. Whether it's knowing which fork to use at the lunch table or how to introduce people at a cocktail reception, entertainment etiquette should not be feared, but embraced. My goal is to put you at ease so you're not anticipating an event with fear in your heart, wondering, "How am I going to get through this?"

As a former society caterer, I know there are two important rules to follow when entertaining:

1. Make sure everyone has a drink in hand.

2. Make sure everyone has someone to talk to.

Believe it or not, these two tips are more important than the décor, the music or the food being served. At any gathering you host, if you can just make sure people feel comfortable, relaxed and connected with others, your event will be a success.

Another thing to consider, before you entertain, is the shopping. I find the biggest mistake people make is that they wait until the last minute to prepare. If you know you are going to have a party in two weeks, buy items for your bar ahead of time. A professional butler would be dead from exhaustion if he we were to try to prepare every aspect of a party on the same day.

I used to have a small apartment on the Upper West Side of Manhattan. My apartment, like many in Manhattan, had a tiny kitchen. Cooking meals for a crowd was a serious challenge, especially given that I had only a little bar fridge—and it was in my home office, not in the kitchen! As a former caterer and as a butler, I studied my space and came up with a formula that allowed me to entertain as though I had a big flat on Park Avenue.

My first rule was to never greet guests at my apartment door. When guests would call from downstairs, I would buzz them into the building and meet them in the hallway at the elevator outside my apartment. I would welcome them there and take their coats and any parcels, so that by the time I opened my door and they entered my home, the preliminaries had been taken care of. I also contained the clutter immediately by using my office as a cloakroom. Next, I found a perfect little spot in my living room where I set up a self-serve bar. My second rule was to pour guests their first drink. After that, I invited each guest to help himself or herself to the handy, self-serve bar.

When it comes to food, people always have the best of intentions, but unless you can cook throughout the party, complicated menus either fail (nothing ever goes as planned when you're in a rush), or you as the host resent the work because you spend all your time alone in the kitchen. No one wants that—not you and not your guests—so what's the best way to deal with this problem? If you can't hire professional caterers, that's okay.

Instead, prepare a buffet menu that is easy both for you and your guests. While working at the famous restaurant Fenton's in Toronto, I learned how to prepare cheese trays that were attractive, interesting and delicious. When I entertained for small or large groups, the cheese board was the centrepiece of my coffee table. I prepared it ahead of time so that the work was done, and the board included a variety of soft, medium and hard cheeses, from mild to strong. I made two boards in advance, so that when the first one started to look messy and picked over, I could do a quick swap and present a fresh platter.

I would design the entire buffet around one hot item, such as a beef stew or a quiche. The other foods were served at room temperature. This made my job easy because I could lay out the entire table before guests arrived and then spend my time with them, rather than fussing with the food. For lunch or dinner, the additional items on the table would include salads, pâtés, smoked salmon, fresh fruits, cakes, miniature pastries and so on. A typical breakfast buffet at my house would include fresh fruit, pains au chocolat and croissants, cheese and crackers and meringues.

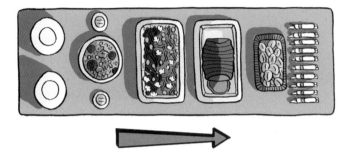

Part of the secret to my entertaining success was that I turned my Canadian antique dining table (which could hold only four or five comfortably) into a buffet table. My apartment living room could then hold ten to twelve people, and everyone would have a place to sit. And all of the food that I served had to be what I call "fork food"—food easily eaten with just a fork and no knife. I would write the menu on a card, so guests would know what had been set out and what was still to come.

When you host any kind of gathering, it is important to watch your guests and ensure that they are having a good time. Do they have a drink? Do they appear to be enjoying the company of those they're talking to, or do they need to be rescued? I believe that as a host you can never totally relax. That doesn't mean you can't enjoy your own party, but to make it a success you need to attend to your guests, and this attention is what allows them to relax and have a great time. That said, when an element of your party goes awry (which it often does), don't show your frustration. As the host or hostess, you are the only one who knows exactly what the party was supposed to look like; if you share your anxiety with your company, everyone will realize that you've made a mistake.

Also, don't be a snob. If you know certain rules of etiquette but someone in your home does not, it is rude and inappropriate to advise them and make them feel uncomfortable. Always be kind and gracious even when others are not.

And finally, whenever I entertain, I like to have bunches of fresh flowers, pleasing background music (at a low volume), and, no matter what, I organize myself so that I have thirty minutes before guests arrive to sit in my living room and relax—ideally with a drink in hand. If you can do all this, I guarantee your party will be a hit! When it comes to entertaining, whether you are the host or the guest, you have a role and a responsibility. In this section of *The Pocket Butler* we will look at how to contribute to creating a successful social event— and I'll even give you hints as to how to welcome an unexpected overnight guest. Hopefully, knowing some of these rules and tips will help you and your guests to feel more at ease in every situation.

HOST AND HOSTESS GIFTS

Personally I find the obsession with host and hostess gifts unnecessary. When I have been a guest at someone's home, I much prefer to wait till after the dinner and send a bouquet of fresh flowers with a handwritten note. The host and hostess might actually have a moment to enjoy them!

Gifts can create a kind of social stress. Should the recipient open them right away? Should flowers be displayed right away (which means scurrying away to find and fill the right vase)? Should the host and hostess serve the wine and chocolates that their guests brought? Should gifts be displayed and announced in front of other guests? Does the host or hostess need to send a thank-you note to guests for their presents (resulting in guests' and hosts' thank-yous crossing paths)? To avoid these conundrums and others, I say, if possible and appropriate, give the gift after the party instead of during it, and keep the gift simple. Even a handwritten thank-you note is a lovely way to express gratitude. Also, consider giving the host or hostess a truly memorable gift that will be used over and over again instead of discarded—a copy of this book!

DRESS CODE

When we are dressed appropriately, we feel good about ourselves and we put our best foot forward. And yes, the little black cocktail dress (for women) and the navy suit (for men) are ideal garments to have in your wardrobe.

I remember going for lunch at the York Club in Toronto. I was young and foolish, and I arrived without a jacket. Who knew you had to have a jacket for lunch? I certainly did not. I was terribly embarrassed. Not only was I barred entry, but the person who invited me abandoned me at the front door and went in for lunch by himself. I never made that mistake again, and wherever I'm dining, I make sure to have a jacket on hand! Depending on local customs, a country's national dress is also appropriate attire for formal functions.

BUTLER'S TIP
If, while hosting, you receive flowers, make the effort to display them in a vase. You can always trim and arrange them properly the next morning.

DRESSING GUIDE BY OCCASION

Invitation Term	Men	Women
White Tie	Black tailcoat, matching trousers with a single stripe of satin or braid in America or two stripes in Europe, white piqué wing-collared shirt with stiff front, white vest, white bow tie, white or grey gloves, black patent shoes and black dress socks.	Formal evening gown.
Black Tie	Black tuxedo or dinner jacket, white French-cuffed formal shirt, bow tie and cummerbund or vest, white silk or linen handkerchief in the breast pocket (optional), black socks, black patent leather shoes. A white dinner jacket with black trousers is perfectly acceptable in the summer, or on a cruise.	Formal evening dress or cocktail dress.

Invitation Term	Men	Women
Black Tie Optional	Many men view this as a welcome opportunity to wear formal attire. A navy blue or black suit with a white French-cuffed dress shirt and an elegant tie is appropriate.	Formal evening dress, cocktail dress or dressy separates.
Semi-Formal	No chance to sport your tuxedo here. The safest bet is to wear a navy blue or black suit with a dress shirt and tie.	Short afternoon or cocktail dress, or a long dressy skirt and a blouse or top.
Business Attire	Even if you normally conduct your business from a home office wearing a dressing gown, this dress code means a suit, dress shirt and tie.	Women's business suit.
Business Casual	Slacks with an appropriate sports jacket with open-collar shirt. Business casual is a classic, neat and relaxed look, yet still professional. When in doubt, err on the conservative side.	Reasonable-length day dress, neat and pulled together separates such as skirt or slacks with appropriate blouse or top, or a pantsuit.

Note: If you have a pet, be sure to check yourself over for hair whenever you leave the house. Keep a miniature lint brush on hand, and even if you miss a few stray hairs, you'll be able to remedy the situation quickly.

TABLE SETTING BASICS

Setting a table can be fun, and whenever possible I like to do it ahead of time, even for simple functions, so that I don't tire myself out just before my guests arrive. When it comes to "tabletop design," as the "fancy people" like to call setting a table, the fashion is simple and elegant. No matter what kind of home you have, you want a table to be inviting for your guests and to reflect your personal taste and style. I've been to a dinner party where the host put three simple Granny Smith apples on a wooden tray in the middle of the table with lots of little votive candles around them. This was the centrepiece, and it looked as beautiful as any gala floral arrangement at a fine hotel.

Sadly, the days of owning many different sets of china are gone, mostly because our homes are smaller and very few of us have a household staff who can polish silver and tend to the different sets of plates. Consequently, it's best to keep your flatware and china simple. This will allow you to mix and match it with different centrepieces, flowers, tablecloths and napkins. I love white dishes for this very reason. As a butler and as a host, with these I can make a table look unique and appropriate no matter what the event.

Before you begin, think carefully; make decisions first, before actually doing anything. When we act without thinking ahead the end result is often less than perfect.

Consider the following details:

• What is the purpose of the meal? Is it formal or informal; a meal for family or for business associates?

• How many guests will attend?

• What is the size of your table?

- What menu would work best? How many courses?

- Will your dinner be plated in the kitchen or served at the table?

- What is the style of your home, and of your flatware and tableware?

Take a methodical approach towards setting the table, beginning with an individual place setting and making sure every detail is in place. Once you are satisfied with your efforts, set the rest of the table. In the end, your guests will notice and appreciate the overall effect.

CHINA

China manufacturers use no universal sizes or standards; however, here are some guidelines for purchasing china or planning which pieces to use for a reception.

- Styles of china can be mixed as long as they are complementary and work well together.

- Plates of different shapes have different purposes and are suitable for different food items. When combining different plates and patterns, think about the effect for the person sitting at the table.

- Consider how plates will work for service. Plates with low rims are more difficult to clear, especially if set on chargers—a flat, decorative plate that sits under the dinner plate.

PLATES

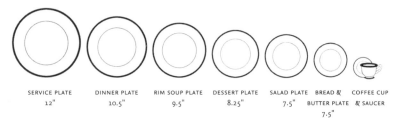

| SERVICE PLATE 12" | DINNER PLATE 10.5" | RIM SOUP PLATE 9.5" | DESSERT PLATE 8.25" | SALAD PLATE 7.5" | BREAD & BUTTER PLATE 7.5" | COFFEE CUP & SAUCER |

COFFEE AND TEA SERVICE

| COFFEE POT | COVERED SUGAR BOWL | MILK OR CREAMER | TEAPOT |

BUTLER'S TIP

If you have spent a lot on dishes, store them properly! Place
felt liners or napkins between dishes to prevent scratches.

SERVING DISHES

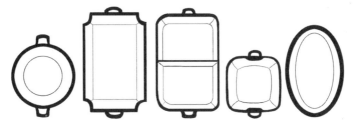

Left to right: CHOP PLATE (FOR PORK, LAMB OR OTHER CHOPS), RECTANGULAR TRAY WITH HANDLES, DIVIDED SERVING DISH (USUALLY FOR SERVING TWO KINDS OF VEGETABLES), SQUARE CAKE PLATTER, OVAL PLATTER

SERVING BOWLS

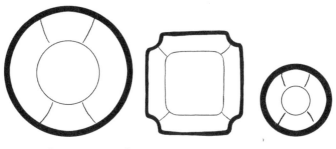

LARGE BOWL (SALADS AND VEGETABLES)   DEEP SQUARE BOWL   SMALL ROUND BOWL

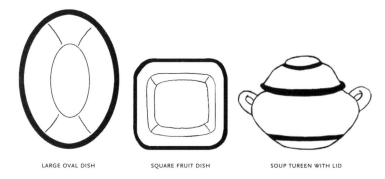

LARGE OVAL DISH   SQUARE FRUIT DISH   SOUP TUREEN WITH LID

CUTLERY

From the days when everyone used to carry around a knife and spoon to parties, to today, when the host or hostess has a full set of cutlery, here is an illustration of all the pieces you need to know.

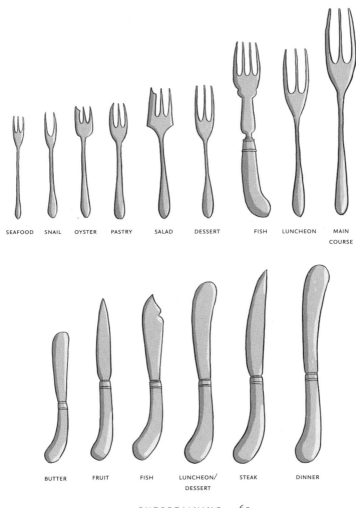

SEAFOOD   SNAIL   OYSTER   PASTRY   SALAD   DESSERT   FISH   LUNCHEON   MAIN COURSE

BUTTER   FRUIT   FISH   LUNCHEON/DESSERT   STEAK   DINNER

SERVING UTENSILS

Left to right: MEAT FORK, FISH FORK, FISH KNIFE, PASTA SERVER, PASTA FORK, PASTRY SERVER, CAKE SERVER

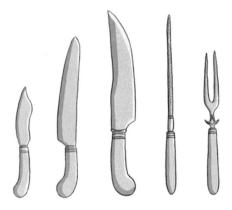

Left to right: BUTTER KNIFE, CAKE KNIFE, KNIFE AND STEEL, CARVING FORK

GLASSWARE

Glasses for red wine tend to be larger than those for white wine and they also have a wider belly, allowing the bouquet of the wine to mix with the air. If you can't tell which glass is which, place them side by side. The larger glass is usually for red.

RED WINE
16 OZ

WHITE WINE
12.5 OZ

CHAMPAGNE FLUTE
8 OZ

STEMMED WATER
GLASS 14.5 OZ

ICE WINE OR
SHERRY 4 OZ

COLLINS GLASS: This is traditionally used for a Tom Collins or iced tea. This glass is very tall and narrow.

 HIGHBALL GLASS: This is the most commonly used glass for large mixed drinks.

 DOUBLE OLD-FASHIONED: This is the most commonly used glass for smaller mixed drinks, or for liquor served either on the rocks or straight up.

BUTLER'S TIP

The bigger the glass, the more people drink. If you want to be economical, use smaller glasses.

HOW TO HOLD A DINNER KNIFE AND FORK

Knowing how to properly hold and use cutlery is an important aspect of proper table manners. The tips and illustrations that follow will show you how.

Place your forefinger on top of the knife. This gives you more control of the knife when cutting food.

With the tines facing down, hold the fork in a similar fashion as the knife, by placing your forefinger on the fork handle. This will give you more control when you spear the food.

Never hold the fork with a clenched fist. It is not a pitchfork!

Never hold the fork by the tip of the handle. You won't have a firm enough grip.

TABLE-SETTING PROCESS

While fashion in table settings has changed over the centuries, affecting the flatware, glassware and china we use, the method of setting a table remains exactly the same.

This is the basic method I recommend:

1. Set just one place setting first. Don't try to set the entire table at once as there will only be more to undo if you don't like how it looks. Make sure the placement is correct and that you are happy with it.

2. Next, take the rest of the chargers or main course plates and place them around the table where you want to position all the other place settings. Keep the spacing between settings equidistant. Once they are properly positioned, organize utensils and glassware around them.

3. Check for symmetry. Why do we care so much about this? Because the human eye loves symmetry. When things are not symmetrical our eye sees imperfection. Use the butler stick for this! (See page 76)

THE NORTH AMERICAN PLACE SETTING

In this table setting, the glasses form a diamond shape above the cutlery, with the first glass placed directly above the main course knife (inside, right). The dessert spoon and the fork are at the top of the plate, and above them is the place card. Guests use the cutlery from the outside moving in. This place setting starts with a soup course (spoon, outside right), moves on to a salad (fork, outside left), a fish course (middle fork and knife) and a meat course (inside fork and knife).

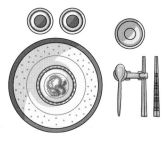

THE ASIAN PLACE SETTING

In Asia, unlike the Western world, there is no standard for formal place settings at tables. In fact, the focus is on the food rather than the place setting. The diagram shows a typical place setting, but it can easily be changed to suit your needs without making any errors of etiquette.

BUTLER'S TIP

A trend in Asian table settings is to provide two sets of chopsticks: an inner set for personal use, and the outer set to be used by guests when helping themselves to communal food.

USING A BUTLER'S STICK

One of the first rules of formal table setting is the 24-inch rule. This refers to the ideal amount of space from the centre of one plate to the centre of the next plate, allowing each guest plenty of elbow room. You may need to decrease the distance if your table is not large enough to allow 24 inches between settings.

The ideal distance from the back of a chair to the edge of the table is also 24 inches. This allows guests to sit comfortably. A good butler will use his or her butler stick to take these two measurements.

Today, few people use butler sticks to set their daily dinner tables, and to be truthful, even the contemporary butler doesn't necessarily use the tool every day. But when there is a special occasion—such as an important family birthday or anniversary—the butler stick can be of use.

This is how a professional butler would set the dining table with a butler stick.

STEP 1:

Align the bottom of the butler stick with the edge of the table. The baseline for a place setting should be about one inch from the edge of the table—the width of the butler stick.

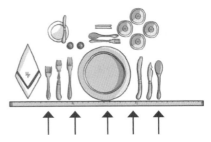

STEP 2:

Align all the cutlery, the plate and the napkin to touch the top of the butler stick. This will create the perfect straight edge for your place setting. The plate should be centred at the 0, the centre of the butler stick.

STEP 3:

Ideally, place the first knife 1 to 1.5 inches away from the plate. Continue using this same metric for the rest of the cutlery so that it is all equidistant. You may choose to reduce the amount of space between items of cutlery if your table space is limited. What's important is to keep everything consistent.

STEP 4:

As you move around the table creating each place setting, use the same measurements.

STEP 5:

To help achieve a beautiful place setting, strive for accuracy, and horizontal and vertical symmetry.

NAPKIN FOLDING

In Victorian and Edwardian times, fancier napkin folds were the mark of well-trained and sophisticated household staff. As the hotel industry flourished in the twentieth century, fancy napkin folds remained important and continued to suggest refinement. This was one of the ways hotels mimicked the sophistication of aristocratic estates.

As beautiful as these napkin folds are, the modern trend is towards a simpler style. In fact, overly intricate folds may be seen as a sign of a lack of sophistication, and even as unhygienic: a professional butler will do everything in his power to avoid touching your napkin, and that includes keeping the fold as simple as possible. Wait staff in modern restaurants, however, sometimes place napkins on the laps of their patrons. This difference in etiquette is one that tells me whether someone has been trained by a hotel or in a butler school.

Having said this, there are some beautiful napkin folds that are appropriate for special occasions. Illustrated here are three folds that I use regularly. My all-time favourite, a fold I use over and over for its simplicity and elegance, is the monogram napkin fold.

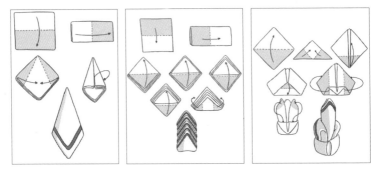

MONOGRAM   **CHEVRON**   **FRENCH LILY**

MENU CARDS

I often notice that when people see a menu card on
a table they immediately think that the meal is very
formal. I see menu cards not as a formality but more
as a really great communication tool for your guests, to
explain what the menu is all about. Because menu cards
generally tell you how many courses the meal will have
and what drinks will be served, they help to guide you
so that you know to either pace yourself, based on the
number of courses to be served, or enjoy everything on
your plate! For me, I find that the information allows
me to relax and enjoy my meal much more.

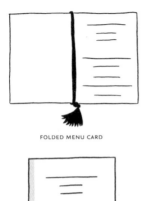

FOLDED MENU CARD

FLAT MENU CARD

HOW TO CORRECTLY WRITE A MENU CARD

The simple format of a menu card has not changed over time. When writing a menu card, keep your language clear. It is pretentious to use foreign-language descriptions on an English menu card unless citing the proper name of a dish—for example, *coq au vin*. Menu cards may be printed or typed. For personal events, they may even be handwritten.

HOW TO PREPARE A CHEESE PLATE

Cheese is more popular today than ever. Although cheese was commonly served at the dining table as its own course, the relaxed formalities of today mean the cheese course at the dinner table is rather rare. It has now become popular during the cocktail hour at parties.

Cheese as part of the hors d'oeuvres course is wonderful. Once served it does not require any further effort from the host or hostess, and guests can help them-

selves. The most important detail when serving cheese is to serve it at room temperature! Most cheese plates have just come out of the refrigerator and are too cold. A cold brie has no flavour, but a room-temperature brie that has been out of the refrigerator for a few hours comes alive and is a delicacy. Cheese will not go bad quickly, so don't worry about that. When slicing cheese for yourself, include both the heart and the rind so that every-one gets an equal share of the various flavours.

The way cheese is served largely depends on its shape. Here are some sample cheeses and recommended methods for cutting.

BUTLER'S TIP
When adding bread to a cheese plate, cut just a few slices at a time. Bread can go stale quickly, so leave out the loaf and a cutting board for guests to help themselves.

Pont-l'Évêque

A square cheese, this has a white-orange rind and is rich and soft, with a creamy, full-bodied flavour.

Tomme

Tomme can be made from cow's milk or goat's milk. The taste varies from nutty to citrusy depending on the type of milk used. The texture ranges from semi-soft to crumbly.

Brie

This cow's milk cheese has an edible, soft white rind. The taste ranges from light and delicate to rich and buttery.

Camembert

This traditional French cheese from the Normandy region has a soft edible rind with a delicate nutty and mild salty taste.

Picodon

This soft goat's milk cheese from the Rhône-Alpes region has a mild flavour. With age, the texture becomes crumbly and the flavour more pronounced.

Valençay

A pyramid-shaped goat's milk cheese, Valençay has a smooth and dense texture, with a mild lemony taste.

Epoisses

Made in the Burgundy region of France, this pungent, creamy-textured cow's milk cheese is rich and salty.

Emmental

This traditional Swiss cheese has a firm, smooth texture with a mild to nutty flavour.

When you make a cheese platter, you should present a variety of soft cheese (such as brie) and hard cheese (such as an aged cheddar). Include a mild cheese as well (such as Valençay), and a strong or sharp cheese (such as blue cheese). You won't be able to dictate how your guests sample your cheeses, but when eating cheese yourself, always start with the mildest variety and work towards the strongest. Going the opposite way may overwhelm your palate, and you won't be able to enjoy the milder flavours.

A beautiful cheese plate presentation says everything about you as a host. Small plates and cocktail napkins are always appealing. Set out one knife per cheese, fresh fruit (grapes, for instance), and plenty of complementary breads or crackers. Whatever breads or crackers you provide should be fresh. If possible, identify the different cheeses.

THE PERFECT BAR

These are the two worst things that can happen when you've set up a bar: a) you run out of alcohol or mix, and b) you run out of ice. Make sure you have enough of each.

Here is a good basic checklist to help you. Remember, every party crowd is different, and you should feel free to make changes based on your guests. You know their drinking habits better than I do! I leave the brands to your discretion.

The quantities on the next page are suggested guidelines for a four-hour cocktail party with 50 guests. Generally, you should plan for 2 drinks per person for the first hour and 1 drink per person for each hour after that. And over the course of the evening, I've found that each person will consume approximately 2 lbs of ice.

BAR SET-UP FOR 50 GUESTS

- ❏ Rye, 1 bottle
- ❏ Scotch, 1 bottle
- ❏ Rum, 1 bottle
- ❏ Vodka, 2 bottles
- ❏ Gin, 1 bottle
- ❏ Whisky, 1 bottle
- ❏ Vermouth—dry, 1 bottle
- ❏ Vermouth—sweet, 1 bottle

- ❏ Wine—white, 10 750mL bottles
- ❏ Wine—red, 6 750mL bottles
- ❏ Champagne/sparkling wine,
       4 750mL bottles

- ❏ Orange juice, 4 litres
- ❏ Tomato juice, 2 litres
- ❏ Cranberry juice, 2 litres
- ❏ Pink grapefruit juice, 2 litres

- ❏ Cognac, 1 bottle
- ❏ Baileys, 1 bottle
- ❏ Grand Marnier liqueur, 1 bottle
- ❏ Cointreau, 1 bottle
- ❏ Coffee liqueur, 1 bottle

- ❏ Water—sparkling,
       24 12oz bottles
- ❏ Water—flat, 48 12oz bottles

- ❏ Cola, 6 litres diet and
       6 litres regular
- ❏ Ginger ale, 4 litres
- ❏ Soda water, 3 litres
- ❏ Tonic water, 6 litres

- ❏ Ice, 100 lbs
- ❏ Olives, 16 oz
- ❏ Lemons, 6
- ❏ Limes, 12

DECANTING WINE

When serving wine in your home, first uncork and taste it, preferably away from your guests. If the bottle passes muster, you can then decant it and prepare it for the table.

STEP 1: Stand the bottle up for a few days before opening to let any sediment settle to the bottom.

STEP 2: Holding the bottle gently, use the cutter on your corkscrew to remove the top of the foil.

STEP 3: Insert the tip of the corkscrew into the middle of the cork and then turn the handle until the screw won't go any farther into the cork.

STEP 4: Move the lever arm down, so that it is flush against the neck of the bottle.

STEP 5: Pull up on the handle firmly to remove the cork.

STEP 6: When decanting the wine, position a light source (like a flashlight, or, if you want to be romantic, a candle) below the bottle—that way, you'll see when the sediment is about to reach the lip. That's when you stop pouring.

POPPING CHAMPAGNE

STEP 1: Remove all of the foil from a well-chilled bottle of champagne.

STEP 2: With your thumb placed firmly on top of the cork, twist the wire cage until it opens.

STEP 3: With your thumb still firmly on the cork and wire cage, slowly twist the bottle from the base with your other hand until you feel the cork release. As fun as it may seem, you are aiming to avoid the dramatic "pop" that results in overflow and loss of champagne.

STEP 4: Pour a little of the champagne into each flute. This is called "priming the glass."

STEP 5: Let the bubbles subside before you fill the rest of each glass 3/4 full.

BUTLER'S TIP
Use the communal
butter knife to take
butter from the butter
dish, and put it on
your side plate.
Return this knife to
the dish, and use
your butter spreader
to dress your bread.

PREPARING TO EAT

When you sit down at any table to "break bread" with family, friends or business associates, there may be a little tension or hesitation before you begin. Perhaps you are thinking: Should I place my napkin on my lap? (Yes.) Can I start the soup, or do I need to watch for someone else at the table to begin first? (No, you'll want to wait for the host or hostess.) Can I finish my glass of water because I'm really thirsty? (Of course!) What do I do if I need to use the washroom during the meal? What if I absolutely must answer my cellphone? (In both of these situations, you'll excuse yourself quietly and leave the dining room.)

No matter what type of table you are at—formal or casual, lunch or dinner—these simple ideas may help.

USE YOUR NAPKIN PROPERLY

When you sit down, put your napkin on your lap. The folded seam should face away from you and the open edges face you. When you need to wipe your mouth, do so on the inside of the napkin and then fold it in half again, with the open edge facing you. Why? Because this way, any grease or dirt on the napkin remains hidden from view and it won't stain your clothes.

USE CUTLERY IN THE RIGHT ORDER

No matter where you are in the world, start by using the cutlery farthest from your plate and work your way inwards towards your plate, course by course.

WAIT FOR YOUR HOST OR HOSTESS

Never start your meal before the host or hostess unless he or she asks you to please begin eating.

WHEN IN DOUBT, WATCH THE HOST OR HOSTESS

Whenever you don't know what to do, never look at the person beside you; instead, look to the host or hostess. It's their table, so they will know what utensils to use.

BUTLER'S TIP

If you drop your cutlery at a restaurant or at a formal dinner, leave it on the floor and ask the server to please bring you a new piece. It is considered unhygienic for you to pick it up.

TAKE PART IN THE CONVERSATION

Although you are there to enjoy your meal—and you should— remember to speak with the diners on either side of you. Don't be afraid to voice an opinion or share a funny and relevant story, provided it is not indiscreet or insensitive.

POLITE TABLE CONVERSATION

"Turning the table" was once a common term and practice. When a gentleman sat at a dinner table, ideally he was responsible for entertaining the ladies to his right and left. He would start by engaging in polite table conversation with the lady to his right (the one he had helped to seat). Halfway through dinner, he would "turn the table," meaning turn his attention to the lady on his left, and converse with her for the remainder of the meal. In today's society, many have lost the art of conversation and our attention spans are short, yet "turning the table" is still a valuable skill. It encourages everyone seated at the table to interact and leads to an enjoyable meal.

Being able to converse about a variety of subjects is important too. You may be an accomplished lawyer or an expert on hydrangea plants, but that doesn't mean these are topics other people want to hear about. A welcome guest is someone who has knowledge of many topics and shows interest in topics raised by others at the table, in order to carry on a civilized and engaging conversation.

But how do you master the art of conversation? First, make an effort to speak with those on either side of you, and at a normal volume. Yelling at a dinner party will dominate others' conversations—and it's a mark of poor etiquette all around. Second, if you're lost for conversation subjects, say something flattering to your neighbour. Don't gush with false flattery, but find something kind, gracious and sincere to say. Third, come prepared with something to speak about. I recommend reading the newspaper every morning, especially before an important dinner. Alternatively, listen to the news on the radio or on television. Doing so keeps you abreast of current events, and will give you many relevant topics to converse about.

TOP TEN RULES OF TABLE MANNERS

1. Your Dinner Napkin: Never tuck your napkin into your collar. When you want to use your napkin, put your cutlery down first and pick it up from your lap. When you are done with your napkin, place it back on your lap and resume eating.

2. Elbows: As your mother always said, no elbows on the table. Also, don't let your elbows stick out at your sides like wings. Keep them tucked into your body, especially when lifting food to your mouth.

3. When You Don't Like What Is Being Served: Inevitably there will be times when you don't like the dish being served. Take a little of what is being served, try it, and try not to look unhappy. You don't need to finish it.

4. Bringing Your Fork to Your Mouth: Never lean over the plate. Instead, bring your fork to your mouth.

5. Your Cutlery: Speaking while holding your cutlery and, worse yet, pointing with your cutlery while speaking is considered very rude. And avoid holding your cutlery "as if you are going to war," as my mother always says. Put cutlery down while chewing.

6. Reaching: Never reach for the salt. Ask the person beside you, "Would you pass the salt, please?"

7. Speaking: Never speak with your mouth full. I know, you've heard it before, but it bears repeating.

8. Blowing Your Nose: If you must blow your nose, never do it at the table. Excuse yourself and go to the restroom or elsewhere. Be as quiet as possible so you do not disturb the other guests at the table.

9. Dealing with Spills at the Table: If you accidentally spill something, don't make a big deal about it. If there are servers, motion for one of them to bring you additional napkins. Deal with the problem as quietly and quickly as possible. If you accidentally spill something on someone else, resist the temptation to wipe them down yourself. Instead, offer your napkin.

10. Concluding Your Meal: At the end of every meal, the napkin always goes on top of the table, never on your chair. Push your chair back into the table; don't leave it where you got out of it.

BUTLER'S TIP
If a meal is included as part of a job interview, remember your table manners! They're not offering you lunch because they're worried that you're hungry.

AFTERNOON TEA VS. HIGH TEA

The idea for the ritual of afternoon tea is often credited to Anna Maria Stanhope, the Duchess of Bedford. Afternoon tea began in the United Kingdom during the Victorian era and was enjoyed by middle- and upper-class households. Usually served between 3:00 p.m. and 5:00 p.m., it was a means of staving off hunger until dinner, which was served later in the evening. Afternoon tea usually consists of a service of tea, with scones, cakes, pastries and/or sandwiches, and is served on a coffee table. High tea was a more substantial meal, with at least one hot food item, served around 6:00 p.m., and is what we would refer to as the evening meal—dinner. Today, the two kinds of tea are often confused and people frequently use the term "high tea" to refer to an elaborate afternoon tea.

Organizing an afternoon tea is a fantastic way to entertain without fussing too much. If you live in a small apartment, it's much easier to invite family and friends to tea than to dinner, and you avoid having to do a lot of cooking. It's also more economical, while at the same time elegant.

I also find afternoon tea to be a great tool for business entertaining. It's the perfect way to get to know a small group socially, but it still allows you to discuss business in a focused and personal session. In my experience, people relax, and you are able to successfully get things done.

QUESTIONS TO ANSWER BEFORE YOU START PREPARING FOR TEA

- How many guests are coming?

- What time will afternoon tea be served?

- What kind of tea would each person like to drink?

- Is there a specific selection of sandwiches, scones and cakes required or would an assorted tray of these food items be acceptable?

Once you can answer these questions, you are ready to begin preparations. The coffee table is usually set prior to the arrival of your guests. Serve the tea itself only after your guests arrive. When you bring in the tea tray, you as the host or hostess may choose to pour the tea into your guests' cups or you may ask one of your guests to pour. The person who pours the tea may add the sugar and milk or lemon for the guests, or the guests may serve themselves.

The tea tray should be large enough to hold all the tea service components, excluding the food. The food is usually brought in separately; the food can be served on plates and brought in on a tray or served more traditionally on a tiered cake-stand. If the food is served on a three-tiered stand, it is placed in this order: cakes and pastries on the top tier, scones and clotted cream on the middle tier and tea sandwiches on the bottom tier. You may offer to serve guests or guests may serve themselves.

AFTERNOON TEA TRAY COMPONENTS

Preparing a tea tray for afternoon tea may seem a straightforward task, but people often get it wrong because they have not placed all the necessary components on the tray. The tea tray properly set with all the appropriate elements is placed near the host or hostess and is ready for immediate service.

- ❏ Small plates (2)
- ❏ Small forks (2)
- ❏ Small knives (2)
- ❏ Teacup and saucer (2)
- ❏ Teaspoon (2)
- ❏ Sugar bowl (1)
- ❏ Milk jug (1)
- ❏ Lemon slices (2)
- ❏ Teapot (1)
- ❏ Hot water pot (1)
- ❏ Flower pot (1)
- ❏ Napkins (2)

HOW TO BREW A POT OF TEA: TEA BAG METHOD

STEP 1: Warm the teapot with a little hot water.

STEP 2: Swirl the water to heat the teapot.

STEP 3: Pour out the hot water through the spout.

STEP 4: Add one or two tea bags to the teapot, depending on the size. Make sure that the tea bag tag is hanging out to identify the type of tea.

STEP 5: Pour freshly boiled (but not boiling) water over the tea bag.

STEP 6: Place the lid back on the teapot and allow the tea to steep 3 to 5 minutes, depending on the type. Then remove the tea bag so that the tea does not become bitter, and serve immediately.

HOW TO BREW A POT OF TEA:
LOOSE LEAF METHOD

 STEP 1: Warm the teapot with a little hot water.

 STEP 2: Swirl the water to heat the teapot.

 STEP 3: Pour out the hot water through the spout.

 STEP 4: Add one teaspoon of loose tea per cup of water.

STEP 5: Pour freshly boiled (but not boiling) water over the loose tea.

STEP 6: Place the lid back on the teapot to allow the tea to brew 3 to 5 minutes, depending on tea type. Then, either remove the tea leaves or serve immediately after steeping.

COFFEE STYLES

Many people who enjoy coffee are picky about how they take it and even what sort of coffee they drink. Always choose a good, fresh bean, and, if you know how, grind fresh-roasted coffee beans yourself. If that's not possible, opt for good-quality ground coffee, and ask the coffee shop to grind it for you. Coffee beans should always be roasted by professionals because they are very easy to burn. Best to leave it to the experts. There are many styles of coffee and different grinds available. A good host or hostess should be familiar with the various options and be prepared to offer guests a perfectly made cup of coffee.

BLACK ESPRESSO CAFÉ AU LAIT CAPPUCCINO

BLACK: Freshly brewed, percolated coffee served without milk or cream in a coffee cup. Sugar is offered.

ESPRESSO: A concentrated coffee brewed by forcing hot water at high pressure through finely ground coffee. Espresso is served in an espresso cup. Sugar is offered.

CAFÉ AU LAIT: Made with equal parts strong coffee and hot, steaming milk. Sugar is offered. It is usually served French style in a bowl, but can also be served in a large cup. The Italian version of café au lait is a caffe latte, consisting of one shot of espresso with a generous amount of steamed milk (a 1:3 ratio). Like café au lait, it is often served in a large bowl or cup, but can also be served in a glass.

CAPPUCCINO: An espresso-based drink consisting of equal parts espresso, steamed milk and frothed milk. It is always served in a cup and can be dusted with either cinnamon or cocoa powder. You should always ask your guests what their preferences are before dusting with either. Sugar is offered. In Italy, cappuccino is served at breakfast only.

CREATING THE PERFECT GUEST BEDROOM

Sometimes while entertaining, you are called upon to house a guest for the night. In the event that someone asks to stay over at your house unexpectedly, there is no reason why you can't be prepared (though I would caution you to try and avoid imposing on your hosts if you are a guest in someone else's home, if at all possible). The comfort and style of

the guest bedroom is part of your visitor's overall experience and should reflect that of the rest of the house. You want your guest to be able to relax there and get a good night's sleep.

A word of advice: I learned from a former employer that sleeping in a guest bedroom yourself for one or two nights is the best way to notice the little details that can be improved. You can't imagine the things I have noticed by doing this.

Provide the following to create the perfect guest bedroom:

- Extra blankets and pillows

- At least one electrical outlet for cellphones and computer chargers

- An alarm clock

- A phone

- Notepaper, a pen and sharp pencils beside the phone or in another convenient spot in the room

- Internet access

- A good reading light beside the bed

- A radio and/or television

- Light reading material (magazines or favourite books) and/or playing cards

THE GUEST BOOK

A guest book provides the host and hostess with a memento in the form of a record of all the guests who have visited their home or attended events there. You often see guest books at castles, palaces, official government residences, stately homes and large country estates. I have always loved these books; it is so much fun to look back at all the people who have visited over the years. I also believe that guests are honoured to be asked to sign the official guest book of a prominent or important residence.

Here are some tips on using a guest book:

- Purchase an attractive guest book from a traditional stationery supplier.

- Write the name of the occasion and the date at the top of the page. (Entries should be on the right side of the page only.)

- Invite guests to sign the guest book as they leave. (The inviter may be you, as the host, or a designated other.)

- Provide guests with a good-quality pen for signing.

BEFORE YOU GO . . .

FOOD AND WINE PAIRINGS

Barbecues	Well-chilled, crisp whites
	Lightly chilled, young and fruity reds

Chicken

Roast	Chablis
	Pouilly-Fumé
Stir-fry	Alsatian Riesling
Curry	Chilled Lager
	New World Chardonnay
	Anjou Rosé
	White Bordeaux
	Riesling

Desserts

Apple Pie	Sweet German wine
	Sauternes
Chocolate Cake	Orange Muscat
Crème Brûlée	Champagne
	Madeira
	Sauternes
Fresh fruit	Muscat
	Sparkling wine
Tiramisu	Port

Fish

Halibut	Pinot Grigio
Salmon	Chardonnay
	Puligny-Montrachet
Snapper	Sauvignon Blanc

Meat

Lamb	Cabernet Sauvignon
	Old World Chianti
	Red Rioja
Pork	White Burgundy
	Beaujolais
Steak, Grilled	Bordeaux
	New World Cabernet Sauvignon
Steak au Poivre	Zinfandel
Steak, T-bone	Barolo
Oysters, raw	Champagne
	Sancerre

Pasta

Meat	Merlot
	Chianti Classico
Pesto	Sauvignon Blanc
Tomato	Zinfandel
	Valpolicella
Proscuitto	Zinfandel
	Riesling
Quiches	Beaujolais-Villages
	Pinot Gris
	Sauvignon Blanc

Soups

Chowder   New World Chardonnay

French Onion   Southern French Reds like
                   Corbières or Fitou

Gazpacho   Chilled Sherry
                   White Rioja

THE BUTLER'S FOOLPROOF MENU PLANS

	Social Situation	Business Situation
Breakfast	This is an opportunity to create a fun meal without too much fuss. Most of these items can be made or purchased the day before (though you'll want to bake the frittata first thing in the morning). Baked frittata; fresh granola; yogurt; assorted seasonal fruit; a selection of muffins, scones or whole-grain toasting breads; café au lait, espresso, coffee or tea.	A business breakfast should be simple and minimal. Don't let an elaborate menu plan get in the way of a productive meeting. Croissants and pains au chocolat; sweet butter and a few different types of jam; coffee and tea.
Lunch	A big group gathering for lunch doesn't need to be complicated in order to be sophisticated. A salad with protein and lots of veggies can serve as a complete meal for everyone. A selection of crusty breads and rolls; Salade Niçoise; cheese plate; pound cake with fresh berries for dessert.	A business lunch should include foods that are not too heavy or sugary, and that are easy to eat without getting caught in your teeth! A selection of crusty bread and rolls; poached salmon served at room temperature; steamed asparagus drizzled with olive oil, lemon zest and Parmesan cheese; rice pilaf with nuts and raisins; shortbread or other bite-sized cookies for dessert.

	Social Situation	Business Situation
Dinner	When hosting dinner for friends, choose a meal that you're comfortable cooking so you have time to entertain your guests and enjoy their company. Tomato and cucumber salad; herb-roasted chicken; warm fingerling potato salad; sugar snap peas; blueberry crisp with vanilla ice cream for dessert.	This is your opportunity to pull out all the stops and impress your colleagues. But one word of advice—make sure you've tried cooking this meal before the big night! There's nothing worse than burning the roast with your boss scheduled to arrive any minute. Green salad with lemon vinaigrette; roast beef tenderloin; slow-roasted tomatoes; steamed haricots verts; garlic mashed potatoes; pavlova with seasonal fruit for dessert.

COOKBOOKS EVERYONE SHOULD OWN

The Cake Bible by Rose Beranbaum
(New York: W. Morrow, 1988)
I love the breadth of this cookbook. It's an incredible reference for all types of cakes, and if you follow the recipes, it's foolproof.

China Express by Nina Simonds
(New York: W. Morrow, 1993)
I've been a huge fan of Nina Simonds's for years. She makes complex recipes so simple to execute, and she walks you through it step by step.

Essentials of Classic Italian Cooking by Marcella Hazan
(New York: Knopf, 1992)
I do not know of a better Italian cookbook author than Marcella Hazan. I have prepared countless recipes from her book over the years and have never had a recipe go wrong. Count on this book for good family-style cooking, or masterful entertaining.

How to Cook Everything: Simple Recipes for Great Food
by Mark Bittman and Alan Witschonke
(New York: Wiley, 2006)
It's simple. I love this because it tells you, in plain
English, how to cook everything!

Mastering the Art of French Cooking by Julia Child
Simone Beck and Louisette Bertholle
(New York: Knopf, 1961)
There is no better cook or teacher than Julia Child.
I had the honour of meeting her three times and each
was better than the last. You could spend the rest of
your life with only this one book and eat well every
single day.

ACKNOWLEDGEMENTS

To my friends and colleagues: thank you!

Marcus L.H. Dearn

Scott B. Munden

Judy Muromoto

John Robertson

Robert McCullough

Zoe Maslow

Nita Pronovost

Brad Martin

Kristin Cochrane

Cathy Paine

Dan Mozersky

Marilyn Denis

Charlotte Empey

Olivier Crémont

Michelle Crespi

Robert Hickey

Dr. Barbara C. Eastman

Madame Viviane Neri

M. Philippe Neri

Mrs. Dorothy Wolfson